T0146437

FLIRTING WITH DANGER

Hiking the Grand Canyon the Wrong Way

FLIRTING WITH DANGER

Hiking the Grand Canyon the Wrong Way

C. P. Webster-Scholten

FLIRTING WITH DANGER
HIKING THE GRAND CANYON THE WRONG WAY

iUniverse books may be ordered through booksellers or by contacting:

iUniverse
1663 Liberty Drive
Bloomington, IN 47403
www.iuniverse.com
1-800-Authors (1-800-288-4677)

ISBN: 978-1-5320-3448-0 (sc)
ISBN: 978-1-5320-3447-3 (e)

Library of Congress Control Number: 2017915486

Print information available on the last page.

iUniverse rev. date: 10/20/2017

To my wayfaring pals
Muriel, Pat, and Wendel.
Thank you, wherever you are,
for this Grand Adventure.

Acknowledgments

Special thanks go to Muriel Bergman who asked me (with a giggle) to write it all down so she could add it to her memoirs. And of course, having more than one set of eyes is helpful and necessary when recording events close to your heart, so I thank Jill A. Scholten and Dan L. Webster for comments that were both helpful and funny. To find the penstock photo, Dan plowed through dusty boxes in search of an old scrapbook. Our father prepared it many years ago when he worked at the Pump and Power Houses in Roaring Springs Canyon, a 4-plus-mile trek below the Grand Canyon's North Rim. In fact, it was this scrapbook and my father's stories that led me to seek work at the canyon as a teenager.

To my husband, Don Scholten, I offer my thanks for taking me back to the North Rim to revisit some of the places mentioned in this story. Also, I extend my appreciation to Kimber Heaton who provided school and portfolio photos of his father, Wendel Heaton. Graphic artist, Sharon Hamre, created the initial layout for the first five printings of this book, and I am grateful for her expertise. In addition I thank Janet Seegmiller and Paula Mitchell of the Gerald R. Sherratt Library at Southern Utah University who led me to information on Wendel's activities while in attendance. And, finally, I thank Monica Wurm, Barbara Briski, and Lora Spencer who often asked, "Why don't you write a book?"

So I did.

Readers' Comments

"This story is a gripping real-life tale of three teenage girls and their high school graduation gift to themselves of a 25-mile hike. Miracles did happen to these girls because they survived 50 years later to share their enduring trial through the intricately descriptive and entertaining writing of wordsmith Webster-Scholten ... By the time I turned the last page, I felt like I was actually on the trek with the girls and one of their friends. It's an emotional roller coaster with every word you read as the chain of events unfold with the girls' jovial laughter ... to tears of exhaustion with miles left yet to hike without food or water ... [It's a] once-in-a-lifetime experience for others to enjoy."

— *The Spectrum/Daily News, Jennifer Weaver, Bureau Chief, Southern Utah*

"Loved your book! 'Twas mistitled though—you were way past Flirting With Danger. You're truly lucky to be alive. Thanks so much for sharing this amazing tale ... Like you, I have suffered in the canyon from my own foolishness, and it has taught me many lessons—some of them geologic ... some of them about laughing when you feel like crying."

— *Charles W. Barnes, Ph.D., Flagstaff, Arizona, author of EARTH, TIME, and LIFE: An Introduction to Physical and Historical Geology*

"What a great experience and adventure, and at an age when we all think we are bullet proof."

— *Ian & Pat Beiers, Thornlands, Queensland, Australia*

"Wonderful story! The visual pictures conjured up during the reading made it almost like being there. Thanks for the trip."
— *Anita Bell, Cedar City, Utah*

"I really enjoyed your harrowing and fascinating story of your "Flirting With Danger" hike across the Grand Canyon. I read your whole story without stopping—it was that thrilling to see the finish!!"
— *Earle L. Forgues, Calgary, Alberta, Canada*

"Once I started reading it I couldn't put it down. It even brought a few tears to my eyes. You did a marvelous job of telling the story."
— *Kevin Horstman, Ph.D., Tucson, Arizona*

"Wow!!! What an accomplishment ... first having that hiking experience and then writing a book about it. Congratulations! I immediately started reading—couldn't put it down—read it from cover-to-cover—what a story!"
— *Grace P. Irby, Oro Valley, Arizona*

"Amazing story and lucky for all of us that you survived to tell the tale."
— *Joe Pavletich, Aiken, South Carolina*

"Wow! That was quite some adventure ... the book tells it all. In reading it I had the feeling I was with you all the way."
— *Everett S. Schmid, Lake Forest, California*

"What a wonderful book you have crafted. I enjoyed reading it the second time as much as the first!"
— *Lindee Berg, Mountain View, California*

"Awesome book! Love the adventure and that it's a true story"
— *Bailee Nolan, Ripon, California*

I could feel your weariness—and it goes without saying that I will never think of tomato soup and instant mashed potatoes without thinking of your adventure.
— *Wendy Murray, Ph.D., New Harmony, Utah*

"What a great story . . . such high adventure. I guess it's good that you can look back on it with humor. It sounds like it was very serious and could have had a different outcome."

- Albert L. Lamarre, Dublin, California, author of MOUNTAINS, MINERALS, AND ME: *Thirteen years revealing earth's mysteries.*

"Snakes, skunks, and rocky switchbacks: FLIRTING WITH DANGER is the dramatic tale of three young women—fresh from high school graduation—taking incredible risks as they hiked across the Grand Canyon with a young male friend in the summer of 1958. The author's prose is as crisp as the desert night air and the story is as exhilarating as the morning sunrise glinting over the rim of the canyon walls. C.P. Webster-Scholten has created a moving personal account of the sometimes funny, sometimes frightening, but always entertaining adventure."

–*Jeff Sherratt, Newport Beach, California, author of DETOUR TO MURDER and other mysteries*

"We have to let you know how we thoroughly enjoyed your Grand Canyon adventure, Flirting With Danger. What an incredible story! It was literally a cliffhanger all the way. ... The mental images your story provided, combined with the excellent photographs, made for a complete hair raising adventure. We have a new respect for the Grand Canyon and adventurers like you and your friends."

–*Roger and Sandy Brennan, Windsor, Ontario, Canada*

"Thank you for the dramatic chronicle you have written of the strength and character of young people who can survive life's most basic challenges. I know you will always be grateful for the experience that taught you so much and enabled you to see and feel firsthand the resilience of the human spirit."

–*Bessie Dover, Cedar City, Utah*

"I thought Penny's account was as interesting and entertaining as anything I have read about hiking in Grand Canyon. Anyone who has done a hike in the canyon can certainly relate to it, but it's written in a way that I think would be enjoyed by all. One of my favorite Grand Canyon books."

–*Mike Armor, Sparks, Nevada*

"I loved this book! Very well written! A fun story with helpful insight on hiking the Grand Canyon."

—Shane Esplin, Milford, Utah

"I [wanted] ... to tell you how much I enjoyed the book, and I've often told people about it. I don't have any personal experiences to compare to it; I must be about the only geologist who has never been down to the bottom of the Canyon. Thank you for writing [it] and sharing your tale about your experience ... way back then. I think it's a memorable book and can serve either as an inspiration or a warning, or both."

—Peter Modreski, PhD, Denver, Colorado

"Wanted to let you know how much we enjoyed your book--Climbing Grand Canyon the wrong way--we read it to our granddaughter after taking her to the Canyon recently. It was midnight before we finished the book and everyone was captivated. Thanks for writing the book that keeps giving!!!"

—Reid and Jolenne Sherratt, Kanab, Utah

A Grand Idea

I told them that a trip like this could change their lives. Despite my descriptions—grandeur, rushing water, the aroma of reeds and willows at creek side, the rainbow of continuously changing colors, and the sounds of canyon critters—my friends were convinced the trip would be too strenuous. The idea of three high school girls crossing the Grand Canyon on a lonely 25-mile trail, switch-backing down one side and up the other, sounded preposterous. After all, climbing the steps to the second-floor chemistry lab was exercise enough. I was persistent, however, expounding on the fact that I had done it twice before when I had worked two summers at the canyon, and I had lived to do it again. I had even done it without food or water, and if I could do it they could do it. My seemingly perfect, yet illogical reasoning and continuous tongue flapping finally won them over on one condition: I help them get in shape to ensure an easy trek for these sheltered city girls.

We set a departure day for a week after our June 1958 graduation from Fullerton Union High School in Fullerton, California, so we just had a couple of months to prepare for our epic journey. To get in shape, Muriel and I (Penny) began by hiking from my house in Fullerton to the small village of Sleepy Hollow in Carbon Canyon, approximately 12 miles each way. Our route took us through orange groves (where present-day California State University is located), across rolling grassy fields, and up a winding roadway to our destination.

Muriel Byars   *Pat Pabrazinsky*   *Penny Webster*

In addition, Pat joined us every weekend as we drove 20 miles to a beach overlook at Corona del Mar, one of California's most beautiful coastlines. From there we walked up and down the access stairs leading to the warm sand—up and down, up and down, up and down. We walked for the first few days and then started running—up and down, up and down, up and down. Though it seemed like we were traversing at least 1000 stairs, the actual count was more like 300. However, when you're training for the adventure of a lifetime, 1000 steps sounds much more impressive. Up and down, up and down, up and down we jogged, weekend after weekend after weekend. I continually tried to impress upon the other two that "The knees are the first to go, so they must be strong, ever so strong." Up and down, up and down . . .

Our days passed with eager anticipation. I knew I could do it, but could they? Of course they could. Our training was top-notch, albeit intermittent with 5 days between each marathon session and led by an untrained, self-proclaimed trainer—me. But, when you're 17 going on 18 you know you're invincible. You can do anything you decide to do. And, so we did.

And, from here on, the tale becomes more of a shared saga of endurance and survival that includes flirtatious males, an Arizona rattlesnake, a death-defying battle with thirst, unmatched hunger, blistered feet, aching muscles, hallucinations, marvelous surprises, applause, and a tree-top-skimming airplane adventure that ended with a finale straight out of Hollywood—REALLY!

The Adventure Begins

Departure day began as any other day, waking to an alarm that jolted each of us from our warm slumber and dreams of whatever teenage girls fresh out of high school dream about. Our hiking shoes (actually white buckskin oxfords, which were all the style in 1958) were ready next to our respective beds, our clothes were packed, my little cream-colored 1954 Ford Business Coupe (with no backseat) was gassed up, and we were ready to begin our journey

Our plan was to arrive in Las Vegas, Nevada, sometime that evening and stay with my aunt. A later-than-expected departure, however, resulted in a near-midnight arrival in balmy Las Vegas, so we quietly spread our blankets on my aunt's front lawn and slept peacefully. Early

Pajama-clad Muriel in haughty pose, Zion Campground.

the following morning, her neighbors kept to themselves whatever comments they had as they quietly drove out of their driveways and past her blanket-strewn lawn. After feasting on a breakfast kindly served by our surprised hostess, we once again set out on the trail of adventure and headed for Utah's Zion National Park campground, which was slated as our second stop.

3

We arrived at Zion mid-afternoon, deftly erected our tent, furnished our temporary shelter with sheets (it was too hot for blankets or sleeping bags), and began preparing our gourmet dinner: instant mashed potatoes topped with canned tomato soup. If we had been served this strange combination anywhere else, it wouldn't have touched our lips; but here, self-prepared, unsupervised, and eaten under the open sky at a rustic table beside our not-so-fancy tent, it was indeed delectable.

Pat, in shorty pajamas, and Muriel's pajama legs in car, Zion Campground.

As the sun was setting behind the tall formations of ancient sand dunes, a nice convertible pulled into the campsite next to us, and out climbed three gorgeous but boisterous teenage boys. Perhaps they too were looking for adventure. We waved to them, caught their attention, and soon learned that they were too worldly for our taste. They were drinking beer, smoking

Pat with Muriel, inspecting our accommodations, Zion Campground.

Pat with Muriel, breaking camp, Zion Campground.

cigarettes, and making way too much rude commotion for the likes of us. After properly snubbing them, we retired to our tent and strained to listen to every word they said. Their language was crude, their manners horrid, and we giggled as we heard one of them say, "What do you think of those three?" Out of the darkness we heard a sneering reply, "Ah, they're just a bunch of immature prudes." Indeed!

The following morning, we broke camp and loaded the car, noticing that the boys at the next campsite were nowhere around, yet their convertible remained parked where it had been the night before. We huddled together for a moment to plan what we could do to let them know we had heard EVERYTHING they had said! Then it came to us. Just as we pulled out, we leaned into their car and placed a short note on their steering wheel, "Good bye, from the Immature Prudes!" Ah, vengeance is truly a wonderful thing!

Heading east out of the park, we zig-zagged up the highway and through the long and famous Zion Tunnel—a hollow tube over a mile long and comprised of orange-red sandstone with huge windows carved into the walls that overlooked the scenery below. Continuing on, we passed Zion's strangely picturesque Checkerboard Mesa and headed east toward Highway 89 where we turned south toward the canyon and our planned adventure. We passed the turn-off to the Coral Pink Sand Dunes, watching the sign disappear in our rear-view mirror, and made a note that someday we'd come back and visit that landmark as well.

Pat and the cream-colored,1954 Ford Business Coupe, Zion Campground

One last look at campsite before departing, Zion Campground.

On ahead, we saw a sign advertising Moqui Caverns, and we couldn't resist stopping for a few minutes. None of us had ever seen a prehistoric cave before, and the advertising on the sign was compelling enough to make us stop and see for ourselves. We entered the cavern, adjusted our eyes to the darkness, and noticed a few travelers refreshing themselves at a bar. Forget that! We had come to see prehistory! Venturing farther into the darkness, we encountered an empty room with an old piano at the far end. Nothing prehistoric here, we thought, but at the sight of the keyboard and the presence of a captive audience in the next room, we decided it was time to sing. And, sing we did!

I began to play the out-of-tune piano, Muriel began to sing, and Pat began to dance to the rhythm as we delivered our entire repertoire of songs—songs we had chosen months before to fit our individual personalities: *I've Got a Crush on You* (for Pat), *Dream* (for Muriel), *Making Believe* (for me), and *Penthouse Serenade* (for all of us). Our bravado continued through the grand finale, which culminated with Muriel belting out her special song, *Summertime*, at the top of her voice as only Muriel could do. With the echo in the cavern and her angelic yet operatic voice resonating throughout all the open spaces of the sandstone cliff, the words were like magic from an unknown, unexplored universe.

Sign advertising Moqui Cave (old Moqui Caverns).
Photo by Donald B. Scholten, 2006.

As she reached the last notes, the ensuing hush was interrupted by applause from somewhere inside the mountain. The thirsty travelers had listened to every note and were yelling "Bravo! Bravo!" as if the performance had debuted that afternoon at the Met! Thrilled, exhilarated, yet somewhat embarrassed, we moved slowly out of the piano room and into the light of the bar where people showered praise upon the three of us and especially our diva. Thus began a career for Muriel that included performances in Civic Light Opera in southern California. To this day, the mention of Moqui Caverns brings smiles to our faces and a longing to return just once more to the wonderful crescendo that preceded the applause of that memorable afternoon. Oh, to hear her sing that song just one more time . . .

Kaibab Plateau

A few miles down the road from Muriel's debut, we entered Kanab, Utah, a small desert town surrounded by more orange-red rock formations, a place made famous by western movies of several Hollywood studios. Our goal in Kanab was to find Wendel Heaton, a friend I had met while working previous summers at the North Rim, and coax him to accompany us across the canyon. He knew every foot of the trail, having worked on it over several summers with his father and their two trail mules. Our search was fruitful, and we were soon headed to the next segment of our grand adventure with a promise from Wendel that he'd "probably be there the day after tomorrow."

Grand Canyon Lodge, North Rim, 1958.

Leaving Kanab, we traveled up onto the Kaibab Plateau and along the winding road toward the North Rim of the canyon. Tall Ponderosa Pine trees stood at attention on both sides of the road, intermittently giving way to broad meadows that dotted the plateau. Arriving at the canyon, we parked near the Grand Canyon Lodge, but I urged Pat and Muriel not to look into the depths until I had led them to the perfect viewing spot.

They stared at the ground as we entered the lodge, feeling

self-conscious and a bit strange that they couldn't see where they were going. I led them through the rustic high-ceilinged lobby, down the stairs, and over to the large windows where tourists often stand for hours watching the changing colors of the incredible panorama before them—the Grand Canyon. When they finally stood at the exact spot where

Bright Angel Canyon from Bright Angel Point, Grand Canyon North Rim.

I wanted them to be, I told them to raise their heads and see what they had come to see. Gasping, they stood transfixed at the view before them. Neither of them had been to the canyon before, and they were astounded at the beauty, the color, the depth, the spirit of what they were seeing. Impressed and thrilled, they stood silently in wide-eyed amazement before finally uttering their genuine delight. Their reaction was all I had hoped for.

We spent the rest of the afternoon wandering around the lodge and along the Rim Trail, stopping at Bright Angel Point and the many other viewpoints nearby. As evening approached, we left the lodge reluctantly and headed to the campground a short distance back down the highway and off on a side road. We established camp, ate dinner, and settled into our tent to discuss plans for the next day.

Morning dawned following a night of slumber as gentle breezes wafted through the tall Ponderosa Pines. Coaxing ourselves out of comfy repose, we prepared for a day of sightseeing on the North Rim, famous for calendar and postcard scenes of canyon depths and astounding color. Point Imperial, Cape Royal, and the Transept Canyon were all on our itinerary, and we visited each one, exclaiming our delight that we would be amidst it all in just a few hours. With night approaching, we returned to camp where we ate and retired once again to rest for the upcoming trek the next day.

Pat at Point Imperial,
Grand Canyon North Rim.
(elevation 8801 feet).

Penny at Point Imperial, Grand
Canyon North Rim.

Pat and Muriel at Point Imperial,
Grand Canyon North Rim.

Penny at Cape Royal, Grand Canyon
North Rim (elevation 7876 feet).

Angel's Window at Cape Royal, Grand Canyon North Rim.

True to his word, Wendel arrived at our campsite late the following morning as we were preparing our essentials for the long trek across the canyon. We packed a bologna sandwich and a candy bar for each of us, and decided not to take water along because, first of all, it was too heavy to carry in our shoulder-strap purse, and secondly, we could drink from the streams along the way. I had done it before, so we could do it this time as well. Waiting for the worst heat of the day to pass, we finally headed for the trailhead, reaching it at about 3:00 p.m., not knowing for sure where we would find ourselves as evening approached, just somewhere down

Wendel Heaton, 1950s. Photo courtesy of Kimber Heaton.

the North Kaibab Trail. We all agreed to alternate carrying the purse between us three girls; Wendel wasn't too keen on carrying such a feminine accessory.

On The Trail

For about the first 4½ miles we hiked happily downward on the steep switchback trail that winds through ancient deposits of limestone, sandstone, and shale, partly shaded by a high alpine forest of Douglas Fir, Aspen, and Ponderosa Pine. We turned onto a short (½-mile) trail for a side trip to Roaring Springs, the water source for the North and South Rims of the canyon. We drank our fill of the cool spring water, and I noted that the volume was not as high as I had remembered from previous hikes. Our thoughts, however, were on the trail ahead and we resumed our trek, passing the old Pump House, making our way down

to the Power House. En route, I pointed out portions of the penstock, a narrow wooden viaduct (with spikes protruding from metal clamps) that carried Roaring Springs water between the two water facilities and upward to the North Rim. I bragged about how other friends and I had walked along that viaduct on previous

Segments of North Kaibab Trail (left and right).

summers, balancing carefully to avoid tripping over the spikes and into the rushing waters of the creek several feet below. I also added that my father had done likewise in the 1930s when he had worked at the Pump House.

Rounding a bend on North Kaibab Trail near Supai Tunnel.

Approaching narrow passage and precipice on North Kaibab Trail.

Mule train on North Kaibab Trail.

*Roaring Springs off North Kaibab Trail, water source
for North and South Rims, Grand Canyon.*

View looking north up Roaring Springs Canyon from North Kaibab Trail.

Penstock between Pump
House and Power
House in Roaring Springs
Canyon. Photo by
Coleby H. Webster, circa 1930.

Power House on North Kaibab Trail.
Photo by Coleby H. Webster, circa 1930.

Wendel Heaton beside Bright Angel Creek (shortly
before water vanished), North Kaibab Trail.

After stopping briefly at the Power House and chatting with the
caretakers, we continued 1½ miles to Cottonwood camp and then
on toward the turnoff to Ribbon Falls, about a mile farther down
the trail. The falls were then accessed by another detour ¼ mile each
way. The path was not steep from this point on, so the walking was
somewhat easier especially with the newly applied bandages affixed to
the sore spots we were now feeling through our thin socks. Though

the afternoon was passing rapidly, the air had become warmer as we descended the trail. The sound of the water tumbling down Bright Angel Creek made us feel cooler as we marched on in the sunshine of late afternoon. Arriving at Ribbon Falls to a chorus of hundreds of frogs, we met our first disappointment. The normally beautiful ribbons of water cascading from a distant source had become instead a trickle that barely made its way over a drying mossy platform into a scant pool of water. Under wetter conditions, the falls would have been more lovely, more voluminous, and the pool would have been much larger than we were seeing now.

Returning to the main trail, we pushed onward along the warm undulating path. It led us through tall stands of willow and other canyon vegetation interspersed with sections where we walked in the now-waning sunlight right beside the streambed that sometimes fell far below the trail. At several points, the trail crossed the creek and we walked across, stepping from stone to stone to avoid getting our now reddish-white bucks wet. However, as we continued on our way, we soon noted that the creek flow was diminishing at our crossings, and then we stared in surprise as we approached another crossing and realized it had disappeared completely. Though slightly concerned at our absent water supply, we remained undaunted as we headed downward toward the steep walls and narrow passageway of Box Canyon. Once there, our next destination would be the campground at Phantom Ranch, which was situated near the banks of the thunderous Colorado River. We knew we would find water there. Phantom was a tourist destination with rustic cabins, running water, and a beautiful rock-lined swimming pool. We could already imagine the quenching delight of that cool, fresh water.

As we continued on, we ate what was left of our sandwiches, having munched on them along the way. The absence of sandwiches lightened the weight of the purse considerably, though at this point a gum wrapper taken from our load would have been noticed. We were tiring and becoming thirstier with each step but eager to reach Phantom. Muriel chugged along, never complaining, unlike Pat and I. The sun had long since disappeared beyond the rim as our descent continued, and we knew the remaining light would soon be gone. The length of the trail from the North Rim to Phantom Ranch was approximately 14 miles, and we had nearly 5 miles yet to go.

Darkness caught up with us as we entered the foreboding confines of Box Canyon, the ancient, steep-walled basement rocks of the canyon that echoed every word and introduced an aura of eeriness to our evening jaunt. Singing was just what we needed to keep our spirits up, so Muriel led us in every song we could think of; even Wendel added his voice to our otherwise feminine strains. As our eyes adjusted to the night, we missed the sound of the creek that had long since disappeared, and all that remained were the sounds of crickets and other small animals. We sang on and on, interrupting our chorus only to comment on the rocks in the trail or the fragrance of the canyon plants that we passed. We sang and laughed and talked boisterously to keep ourselves alert as we weaved our way through the narrow canyon with an overhead moon that helped guide our way.

Rounding a curve in the trail still singing triumphantly, we came to a rapid halt that instantly stopped our song as Wendel yelled, "SNAKE!" There in the middle of the trail a large clump of long narrow flesh was coiled and ready to strike as it made its undeniably recognizable hissing rattle. We could do nothing! It was in our direct path! We were stone silent, immovable, stunned, frightened, rigid, not knowing what we should do next with this mass that was rattling at us about 6 feet in front of Wendel who was in the lead of our previously happy and rowdy procession.

To this day, I'm not certain how he did it without seeming to move, but carefully and slowly with his hands behind his back, Wendel materialized a tissue from his back pocket, lit it on fire with emergency matches, and tossed it toward the snake, hoping the diversion would cause it to strike at the flame instead of our stunned parade. It worked! In one tiny instant, the snake struck at the flaming air and we scrambled backward to safety, watching with horror as the slithering mass writhed and rattled its angry and ominous warning. Quickly scrounging for a long, pronged stick, Wendel maneuvered the creature to the edge of the trail and then over the side to the dry creek bed below, where, undoubtedly, it wound itself back into striking position awaiting other unsuspecting and less raucous prey.

A sobered foursome, we eventually started moving once again, this time with trepidation as our hearts pounded and our feet stumbled onward. Our trek was now quiet and careful as we made our way through the darkness to Phantom Ranch, a place well named to our way of thinking in this ruggedly eerie landscape.

Phantom In The Night

We arrived at the campground adjacent to Phantom Ranch around 10:30 p.m., moving quickly to the water spigots. Unknown to us, a drought had dried up our expected water sources (prior research would have told us that much), and Phantom Ranch was also dry except for water cached for the paying guests, and they were fast asleep in their wonderfully snug and rustic cabins. Even the famous creek-fed Phantom swimming pool was dry.

Realizing our desperation now, we could go no farther. We ate our candy bars, our last bit of food, and collapsed onto the wooden tabletops of a nearby campsite, finding sleep an easy escape from a troubling and increasingly worrisome plight. A good sleep, however, was not ours to enjoy. A family of skunks paraded by and then lingered near our tables, seemingly fascinated by our presence. I began to wonder if skunks would be bold enough to jump onto the tables in pursuit of their fascination. Then I wondered if skunks could even jump. We remained motionless for what seemed like hours, until their curiosity waned and they finally continued along their way. As we breathed deeply and relaxed somewhat from that potentially messy predicament, a new concern emerged. Bats from canyon caves began to dive-bomb us as we waved our arms and swatted at them, trying to keep them away. Realizing that we were out-numbered and outwitted by the canyon critters, we grudgingly figured it was time to be on our way once again. In addition, the intermittent breeze and the hardness of the wooden tabletop beds made us aware that we still had more than 9 miles to reach the South Rim, no more food to eat, and no water to drink.

Reluctantly, we rubbed gingerly on our increasingly painful knees and stiffened joints, and rebandaged our now-blistered feet. Pat and I were more vocal with our suffering, but Muriel remained relatively quiet, never complaining about much of anything. In fact, she had always taken things in stride and was forever cheerful. Our beautiful white bucks had morphed into a reddish-white color and then into just plain dirty bucks—not exactly appropriate footwear for rugged hiking—but remember, the year was 1958 and we were invincible. With no solution to our thirst and hunger, we arose from our temporary resting places atop the wooden tables and slowly moved on once more.

It was about 1:00 a.m. as we rejoined the trail leading away from Phantom's campground. We slowly crossed the old Kaibab suspension foot bridge across the Colorado River, trying not to think about the millions of gallons of silty water roaring beneath our feet every millisecond, too thick to drink and too dangerous to reach even if we'd had a mind to give it a try in the darkness. We watched through the heavy metal mesh as the torrent thundered past, a roiling giant serpent ominously illuminated by the moon overhead as it slithered downstream.

Reaching the south side of the river, we took the River Trail westward and trudged along the heavily sanded path for about 2 miles. Tired from the entire day and its disappointing discoveries, as well as our struggle in the deep sand that now defined the trail along the river, we reached Pipe Creek and turned onto the Bright Angel Trail. We trudged away from the river's sound of awesome power and headed inland following the dry creek bed. Before the actual ascent to Indian Gardens camp began, we discovered a small seep at the side of the trail, emanating from an unknown source. Hesitatingly, we moistened our lips and tongues, but doing so provided no real relief to our thirst. Ever on the lookout for more slithering, coiling, scaly reptiles, we hiked more slowly now up the Bright Angel Trail, with over 17 miles behind us (including our side trips) and about 7 miles yet to go to the South Rim of the canyon. It would be the longest 7 miles we would ever travel.

Inching Toward Dawn

The moon was bright as it shined down upon the winding trail. Now devoid of the deep sand we'd encountered along the river, the hiking was easier except it was now all up hill on what seemed like an endless path that wound back and forth through the layers of ancient stone. In reality, this segment was not as bad as we made it out to be. Muriel reminded us of our innocent training days, walking and running up and down our so-called 1000 steps, and we remembered the sound the ocean waves had provided for us, a gentle rhythm keeping lazy time to our eager practice sessions that now seemed like 100 years ago. We had been fresher then; we'd had plenty of sleep; we'd been nourished; we'd been eager; we'd been optimistic; we'd been naive.

But, it was too late to change our minds. We were at the bottom of a mile-deep canyon with miles to go before we slept. Pat and I were beat, Muriel was beginning to tire, but Wendel seemed to show no discomfort. He was used to this trail, though his treks normally took place during the daytime. Still, ever the optimist, he cheered us on with gentle persuasion, telling us that the worst would soon be over and we'd be able to rest a while at Indian Gardens. We heard no complaints from him about his sore feet or aching knees, or thirst, or hunger, or anything else. We didn't want to appear to be helpless females, so we trudged onward and upward, up, up, and up, stopping now and then to catch our breath. At least it wasn't mid-day when the blazing sun would be frying us in 110-degree heat. It was probably in the high 80s or low 90s, but our thirst was growing by the quarter mile. I knew water would be abundant at Indian Gardens. It had been there for generations trickling along an ancient stream that the Indians had used to water their crops in this small inner canyon oasis.

Our eyes played tricks on us as we rounded each bend, carefully watching the trail for dangers of any kind. Did they have mountain lions in the canyon? We dared not think out loud about that possibility. Snakes were bad enough, and we were highly aware that many were, undoubtedly, lurking about. Still, strange apparitions were ever present, and they appeared sinister in the darkness until we finally passed each of them in turn to discover only a jutting ledge of sandstone, an awkwardly shaped tree, or an oddly formed rock formation. One false step is all it would take to disappear over the edge to a crippling fate or worse. We had to concentrate. We had to use our heads and not our imaginations. We had to go on. If only we had something to drink and something to eat—anything! Did snakes really taste like chicken?

Our pace was slow and we finally reached Indian Gardens sometime before dawn, parched, hungry, dog-tired. We needed sustenance! We needed water! We needed sleep! We needed a miracle! The water spigots didn't work here either though we turned the handles again and again. Nothing! Over and over again, back and forth we turned them, but the water was non-existent. Mustering all the strength we had, we nearly fell over each other as we stumbled to the ancient brook that runs alongside the campsites. We were ready to immerse ourselves completely, opening our mouths to let the water pour into us and over us and through us. At this point it could carry us away if it wanted to so long as we could drink it in as we vanished into oblivion. However, this stream too was dry from the same drought that had dried up the water on the north side of the river.

Dry—a word whose meaning we couldn't fathom nor even bear to acknowledge. Five steep miles of nothing but switchbacks awaited us, that is, if we ever moved again, a fact that we now knew wasn't anything to laugh about. Except, we were laughing hysterically, uncontrollably, laughing to keep from crying like helpless females. Wendel said nothing, but we figured he was struggling along with us. For so many miles I had known that we would somehow be rescued from our own stupidity, rescued by the ancient streams that had never let me down before. But they had let us all down this time. Our spirits had ebbed and then had fallen completely, and we were in trouble. Totally exhausted, we again fell into fitful sleep on top of more hard and dusty camp tables, too tired to swat the insects that buzzed around us. Perhaps the vultures would come soon.

Hallucinations

As we awoke, the morning sun was bright, driving its rays through the branches of the trees overhead and into our faces. No escape was possible now from the relentless heat that would soon be upon us. The sun had already moved over the rim to shine down upon the small oasis of Indian Gardens, which was situated at the inside edge of the Tonto Plateau. Muriel looked toward the rim, noting out loud that the sparse shade along the rest of the trail was diminishing faster than we could have walked in the best of condition. We weren't laughing anymore; we were too exhausted to laugh, too sobered by our meager and troubled sleep, and morbidly aware that we still had nearly 5 miles and over 3000 vertical feet to ascend straight up in the intense heat of the day. If we waited until nightfall, we would never make it out.

At mid-morning, with leaden feet, unbearable thirst, and empty stomachs, we headed out slowly, limping ever upward. Our blistered feet and stiff legs were matched by the soreness of our backs and the stinging in our dry dust-filled eyes. Conversation was minimal, though I tried to assure Muriel and Pat that we'd make it even if it took all day. It would be tough, but we were tough, and we'd make it no matter what. With any luck, two rest stops between Indian Gardens and the South Rim would have water fountains. They were provided by the Park Service, and maintained for the casual hikers who rambled into the canyon each day down as far as their brief visits would allow before scurrying back to the rim. In 1958, few of them ever ventured as far down the South Rim as Indian Gardens, and hardly anyone ever crossed the canyon in the middle of the summer—except mad dogs and Englishmen! Water was always present at the rest stops, and sometimes food could be found discarded by optimistic day hikers who usually carried more supplies into the canyon than they were willing to carry out. I almost convinced myself, but at least it kept the rest of the group walking.

Pat, however, was starting to act a little strange, mumbling words we couldn't quite decipher. Our progress was ever slower, the heat was ever hotter, and the trail was ever steeper. The switchbacks were relentless and long—longer than I had remembered from previous hikes. It was taking us longer to move upward. It was taking us longer to do anything. The rim seemed farther away now as the sun beat down in relentless pursuit of the ill-prepared. Even Muriel was visibly wilting and softly questioning our decision to hike the canyon. Only Wendel, ever the nimble-footed gazelle, had found strength somewhere and moved upward urging us along as if we were on a Sunday stroll in New York's Central Park.

It became increasingly difficult to lift each leg to make each step, and Pat would sit down on the side of the trail every few yards, still mumbling to herself. Muriel and I thought at first that she was just being silly because her mumblings would turn to laughter followed by more mumblings. She progressed to sitting in the middle of the trail, refusing to move until she felt better, which took longer each time she sat.

Wendel decided to go on ahead to check the water supply at the upcoming rest stop. We waited for him as long as we dared at every possible waiting place on the trail, but we knew the time we spent waiting was time spent wasting, so we would head out again only to have to stop and rest even more. At this rate we'd be lucky to make it out by sunset if we were still alive by then. I knew Muriel and I would make it, but I wasn't so sure about Pat. She was crying now, and as she moved upward, she began swinging her dangling arms like an elephant swings its trunk, repeating to herself, "I'm so tired, I'm so tired." She continued, "If I just had a mule to pull me out. Run tell Wendel to bring his mules down here so we can ride." She was uttering words now breathlessly with her weakened voice, and was completely unaware that

Wendel had gone on ahead to check on water, and his mules were in Kanab, Utah, 100 miles north of our predicament.

A couple of hours later we reached the first covered rest stop and found the water supply there too had dried up along with all the others. The spigots were stiff, and no one had left any food for us would-be scavengers. We would have been happy for stale bread; we'd have happily wrestled a squirrel for it, but nothing could be found. The Park Service trail crew had already emptied the trash, and any potential stray bit of food was long gone into a dumpster on top of the rim. Oh how far away it seemed now. Three miles more was all we had to go, but it might as well have been 300 miles. Where was Wendel? I assumed he had gone on up to the next rest stop 1½ miles or so up the trail, so again I urged us onward.

Muriel arose from the bench where we had rested, and began inching her way from the fly-buzzing shade of the rest stop back into the direct sunlight. However, it took some time and significant coaxing to get Pat moving again. Eventually, we were all back on the trail and moving upward, one foot in front of the other. Pat began mimicking the sounds of a mule rider— "Yee ha! Yee ha!" —and swinging a make-believe whip in the air making it land on her imagined beast that she fancied was now transporting her upward. Bursting into tears, she kept up the strange mumblings.

We now realized it wasn't a game. She was hallucinating! Muriel and I looked at each other, shaking our heads slowly; our faces were grim. As we quietly discussed how the two of us could carry her out in our condition, Pat uttered what became—and remains to this day—our favorite remembrance. Nearly delirious, with speech becoming more and more difficult, she called out in a series of gasps, "Yee ha! Yee ha! I'm so tired, I can't even say 'Yee ha!'" The three of us collapsed in the middle of the trail and laughed until we were all crying at the nonsensical uttering of our buddy who was, without a doubt, dangerously ill. Life had to get better from here; no other options remained.

As if in answer to her pleas, a maintenance crew working on the trail came into sight at the next switchback, and to our surprise they had a mule with them. It didn't take much coaxing on our part (Wendel had apparently met up with them and described our plight), and they graciously allowed Pat to hold onto straps that hung down from the work saddle of the beast as it pulled her upward. "She can't ride," they said, "because of the liability issue, but we can pull her up for a ways." Half walking and half dragging, she moved slowly upward, expending minimal effort as the trail-savvy mules pulled and pulled our hallucinating friend, who was by now laughing hysterically once more with tears rolling down her dusty face. Seeing her condition more clearly, the crew disobeyed their rigid policy and put her on top of the mule. She held on tightly, hunched over like a wounded soldier returning from battle.

Bear Hug

A few switchbacks more and, from a distance, we spotted what looked like Wendel, but his arms were wrapped in a bear hug around something large. We watched as he drew nearer, and saw that he carried what appeared to be huge, brown bags in both arms. Discovering no water at either of the rest stops, he had hiked to the rim, bought hamburgers and water for us, and had run back down the trail to rescue us all. Chateaubriand could not have tasted as good as those hamburgers tasted that hot, dusty, miserable day. And, Wendel became our instant hero who had saved us once again from certain calamity. Our thanks were totally inadequate as we gobbled the food and poured the water down our heavily parched throats. The mules and their crew continued on their work schedule without us, but we were in better shape now with food and water in our stomachs.

Refreshed, though still incredibly stiff and tired, we continued upward and began meeting people along the trail who were out for an easy stroll into the canyon. "You're the girls who were in trouble," they would say. "How are you doing now?" Apparently, Wendel had relayed our sad tale in response to their questions as he had dashed past them back into the canyon with bags of food in both arms. The four of us were fast becoming celebrities, and everyone we passed was encouraging us onward. Even Pat was re-energized by the well-wishers, and she moved somewhat faster.

A mile or so still to go and the sun was hotter than ever, blasting us with a flame thrower, beating us into soggy, dirty, red-stained, sunburned urchins who limped and drug our bodies as if they were steel weights attached to heavy chains. The food had helped immensely, but we realized that the danger wasn't over. Upward, ever upward we trudged, bedraggled—all except Wendel. He skipped back and forth, urging us onward, teasing us with, "Boy, would a nice ice-cold root beer taste good right now!" We reacted to his goading only half in jest. "Shut up, Wendel, or we'll take back all those nice things we've been thinking and saying about you. Yes, a nice ice-cold root beer would be great right now, but we still have a mile and a half to go and this heat is horrid! You shouldn't keep teasing us like that."

Then, just as he repeated his root beer comment all over again and we began to yell at him once more, he stepped behind a large rock formation beside the trail and pulled out another sack, this time full of nice ice-cold root beers! Somehow he had carried them ALL along with the armload of hamburgers and water, and had stashed them behind the rock, knowing that we would be in dire need once again by the time we reached that place in the trail. He was our savior, a gazelle, an angel all rolled into one! We've never been able to properly describe our feelings for him, and to this day we remember his heroic acts that assisted us helplessly stupid females on that most memorable day.

Finishing the root beers, we were ready for almost anything. The burgers had kept us going, our thirst was quenched once again, and we were nearing the last long switchback. The South Rim was in sight. More and more people were hopping sprightly down the trail and saying all kinds of nice things encouraging us onward. "You're just about there! Nice going! Good to see you all safe!"

End of trail at Bright Angel Trailhead, South Rim, January 2007.
(note snow on trail)

We were amazed even more at our celebrity status when, as we reached the top of the trail and what we thought was the end of our adventure, people who were standing along the rim began to applaud. Stunned, we realized they were applauding for us—the bedraggled four who had endured misery and all manner of discomfort and then had been miraculously saved by one of our own. They were applauding for us and we could hardly speak as tears of relief and gratitude rolled down three of our faces. It was 3:05 p.m., exactly 24 hours and 5 minutes since leaving the cool shelter of the Ponderosa Pines and heading down the hot, steep North Kaibab Trail on the North Rim of the Grand Canyon. We had descended over 5400 feet in elevation from the North Rim, and had ascended over 4400 feet to the South Rim. Including our detours from the main trail, we had traveled over 25 miles to reach our destination.

Incredulity filled our thoughts, knowing that we had all survived the trek largely unscathed, but we also knew that we were sore, weary, and incredibly dirty. Wendel, however, was unaffected for the most part. He had been the strong one all along, though we guessed he was just as relieved to have reached the rim for the second time that day. Sore and stiff, nevertheless, we were all enchanted by the scene as we looked back into the canyon realizing that we had endured it all. The multicolored layers of rock looked like the results of an artist swishing paint-loaded brushes across a panoramic canvas. The beauty displayed there before us was surreal, and in silence we gazed into the depths for a long time, replaying in our minds the events of the past 24 hours.

We continued our wandering along the rim, our strength now miraculously restored, and then spent a lot of time inside Bright Angel Lodge where the padded leather seats felt snug and comfortable as we sat in front of the large but empty fireplace. After a time, we grabbed a bite to eat though our budgets did not allow for the fancy meal that we felt we deserved. And, as night fell upon the rim, we knew we needed to sleep. We hadn't planned on needing lodging, so we had just enough money left to buy food and plane tickets back across the canyon the following morning. Wendel assured us that he had a place where he could sleep (we figured he had some buddies in the wrangler barn and could bunk with them), so Pat, Muriel, and I ventured into the ladies lounge at the lodge, found a couple of couches, and fell into a dead-man's form of sleep. I vaguely recall hearing the door open several times during the night as guests came in to use the facilities, and I remember the sound of water running and paper towels being dispensed, but I couldn't move and my eyes were tightly shut. We slept until a little after dawn the following morning when the cleaning crew arrived and looked at us in disgust. Their somewhat menacing stares made us aware that the nice couches in the ladies lounge were certainly not the appropriate place for the filthy likes of us.

We washed our faces, trying desperately to make ourselves look like the girls we really were instead of the urchins we had become. The efforts were futile, so we limped out of the building in search of Wendel. We found him outside the Bright Angel Lodge, sitting stiffly in one of the large chairs he had drug over from a canyon overlook nearby. He was huddled down tight with his hands in his pockets and his collar up over his ears, trying hard to stay warm in the crisp morning air. Questioning him, we learned that he had spent the entire night in that same chair, repositioning himself frequently and trying in vain to ward off the chill. Though it was June, the night air at 6,800 feet elevation is cooler than one would hope when sitting through it at the mercy of the elements.

Bright Angel Lodge, January 2007.

We ate a small breakfast and went in search of a telephone to call for flight information. We made our reservations, but Wendel said he wasn't sure he was ready to leave yet, and he suggested that we go on without him. After pressing him further and coaxing him to come with us, he admitted that he felt like running back across the canyon. We were stunned once again by his actions. How could he possibly have the strength to walk—not to mention run—back across those rugged and seemingly endless miles? Dumbfounded, we urged him to forget such foolishness and fly with us, but he adamantly refused. We watched as he started back down the trail, indeed loping gracefully, until he was out of sight. In hindsight, we're pretty certain that he did not have the plane fare to cross the canyon but was too proud to say so. Many times since that day, we've wondered if that was really the story. Had he spent all his money to rescue us with burgers and root beer? We would have pooled our money and bought him a $7.50 plane ticket, but he had insisted that he wanted to take the trail back.

Hollywood On The Kaibab

Catching a ride with the local sheriff, we traveled the 10 or so miles to a tiny airport near Tusayan, just outside the Grand Canyon National Park boundary. We boarded the small four-seat sightseeing plane, listened as the engines revved, sat back tightly as the plane moved down the runway, and relaxed into the seats as we rose into the air, circling the runway once before heading toward the rim of the canyon.

Seeing the Grand Canyon from the air in a tiny plane is one of the great thrills of a lifetime. Not only are the colors spectacular, but also the layered depth is magnificent, and when viewed from such a vantage point, a person feels like a bird soaring into a vast, endless, colorful universe. The updrafts from the canyon tossed us about like corks bobbing on a rippling pond, but the experience was exhilarating, and the flight drew to a close much sooner than we would have liked.

We watched the canyon disappear behind us as the plane traveled inland for about 25 miles to reach the landing strip near Kaibab Lodge, just north of the national park boundary. We skimmed over treetops until the small unpaved landing area came into view. The pilot guided the plane over the meadow runway a couple of times to herd the cows from their peaceful grazing, and then we set down on a short, bumpy, dirt path on one of the many picturesque meadows of the Kaibab Plateau. Dust flew behind us as the wheels met the limey, yellow-brown dirt, and then it engulfed the plane as we came to a stop at the end of the makeshift runway. The pilot waited as the dust settled and then carefully opened the door to the cockpit where we deftly emerged, this time each of us feeling like a soldier returning from war in triumph.

Deplaning, we slowly headed out toward the highway so we could hitch a ride from a passerby, as was the custom when people flew across the canyon unless they had prearranged with someone to pick them up. We had no prearrangement, so as we trudged away from the plane toward the road, the pilot yelled that he might have a ride for us. He had just received a message that another party was waiting for the plane to return to Tusayan so they could fly across too, and if we waited here until they landed, we could ride with them back to the North Rim. It was good news so we waited, rambling around the meadow, kicking cow pies, smelling wildflowers, and talking, talking, talking about our adventure and Wendel's seemingly super-human strength.

Meadow runway near Kaibab Lodge. Landing area directly in front of tree line. Photo by Donald B. Scholten, 2006

About an hour later, we heard the sound of the plane motor as it approached the dirt field, and watched as it executed the same maneuver to move the cows off the runway before it landed. Two young boys, perhaps 9–10 years old, climbed out of the passenger side, and they were followed by an older man whom we presumed to be their father. They were all nice looking, well mannered, and cordial as we introduced ourselves, thanking them for our upcoming ride. In our noisy conversation, they asked where we lived. We replied California, and the boys quickly added that they were from California as well. Then, we learned that they lived in Hollywood, and I decided to try to make them feel important. "So are you both a couple of little movie stars?" I asked, fully expecting a bashful denial. "As a matter of fact, we are," one of them answered with a smile on his face. "This is my brother, Bobby, and I'm Johnny Crawford. I play in *The Rifleman*[1] and (motioning to the older man) this is our guardian." We were absolutely shocked as we shook hands with each of them, trying to dispel any indication that we were suddenly in awe of these two famous little stars.

As we waited for their transport, we made small talk and asked if they would give us their autographs. They obliged and politely wrote small messages to each of us on the edges of some Grand Canyon National Park maps that we had acquired from the pilot. One message in particular (I think it was the one on Muriel's map) said something like, "Hiking across the Grand Canyon is pretty good, especially for a girl."

Their transportation arrived, and we climbed inside the relatively small car. The space was minimal, so Bobby and Johnny sat on our laps (I don't remember who sat on which lap), and we headed back to the rim. Arriving at the campground about an hour later, the three of us approached our tent, tired, sore, and stiff, but pleased that our merry but troubled adventure had a true Hollywood ending.

---

[1] *The Rifleman* was a popular television program (1958–1963) starring Chuck Connors and Johnny Crawford. It is considered "one of the great classic western adventure series." Johnny first performed as a Disney Mouseketeer. Bobby later played in or produced several television programs, including *The Californians, Dragnet, Gunsmoke*, and many others.

Marathon

Later that evening as we were finishing our gourmet instant mashed potatoes with tomato soup gravy, a familiar face appeared at our camp. Wendel had indeed run across the canyon and had done it in less than 8 hours. He had jogged about 25 miles—down the upper switchbacks of the Bright Angel Trail; through Indian Gardens; down the lower winding trail along Pipe Creek to the river's edge; through the deep sand along the River Trail; across the Kaibab suspension bridge; past Phantom Ranch; through Box Canyon; past the trail leading to Ribbon Falls; past Cottonwood Camp, past the Power House; past the trail leading to Roaring Springs, the Pump House, and the penstock; up the steep switchbacks of the North Kaibab Trail; onto the staging area at the trailhead; and then down the paved highway for an additional mile to our campsite—all in under 8 hours! Not only was he a gazelle, he was part cheetah.

Wendel stayed with friends at the Park Service dorms that night, and we stayed once more in our own cozy tent. Sleeping

Muriel Byars, Wendel Heaton, and Pat Pabrazinsky at Wendel's home, Kanab, Utah, June 1958.

soundly, we awoke the following morning having experienced more than any of our city friends would ever believe. Smug in our accomplishments, we picked up Wendel and drove back through the Ponderosa Pines of the Kaibab National Forest and eventually back into Kanab, Utah. We waved happily as we drove away, leaving him at his home on a bright, sunny, cheerful afternoon in late June 1958.

Then the little cream-colored Ford headed north up Highway 89 and then westward, driving merrily along the mountain roads, eventually reaching my former hometown, Cedar City, Utah. We spent a few nights there with my relatives, then loaded up two of my cousins and headed back to California. We were three beaming high school graduates, sophisticates from California, experienced canyon hikers extraordinaire, and the cousins were mere sophomores from a small Utah town who did not know how to drive and were male to boot. With no back seat in the Ford, they sat on pillows (on the floor) for over 400 miles, sucking on ice cubes and dropping them down the back of our T-shirts as we sped across the hot Mojave Desert of southern Nevada and southern California. To this day, they admit they've never forgotten their own young adventure riding in the back of the small coupe with no open windows, no seats, no air-conditioning, and three foxy female teenagers in the front seat warning them of the perils of the big city.

Epilogue

More than a half-century has passed since that epic adventure, and the "hikers extraordinaire" have followed divergent paths during that time. Muriel, Pat, and Penny are all in their late 60s (at the time of first publication in 2008) and, hopefully, wiser than the day they headed down the trail. They've raised families, established careers, and shared their laughter along with their sorrows, maintaining the close bonds they made so many years ago. They celebrated Muriel's 65th birthday together where they reminisced with other guests, relating much of this story to those who had never heard it before. Thus the seed of this little book was sown.

Muriel Byars Bergman, mother of four, lives in Fullerton, California, and is an administrator with an international, professional business services company. Her natural talents are in the arts where she excels in painting and writing. She has sold her paintings and has displayed her work in gallery shows. In addition, she has sung in civic light opera performances in southern California and still sings like an angel. Her Grand Canyon hiking, however, remains a one-time performance.

Pat Pabrazinsky Fowler, mother of three, lives in Paso Robles, California, where she is an accomplished and award-winning horsewoman. She raises horses, cares for them, trains them, parades them, and eagerly showers them with love. Before her retirement, she participated in horseshows throughout California. She is happiest riding on horse trails of the Pacific Coast, sometimes making her own trail as she and her horses push their way through the underbrush. She too has not hiked the canyon since June of 1958.

Penny Webster-Scholten, mother of two, lives in Cedar City, Utah, and is a retired geologist and scientific writer/editor. She has hiked over 600 miles throughout the canyon in all kinds of weather and, for the most part, with the appropriate hiking gear and adequate food and water. In addition, she has rafted the Colorado River the length of the canyon (277 miles) through calm waters and wild rapids. Perhaps she'll add yet more miles on the canyon trails before she retires her hiking boots, reluctantly.

Muriel Byars Bergman, Pat Pabrazinsky Fowler, Penny Webster-Scholten, 2008

Wendel Heaton became Student Body President at the College of Southern Utah (now Southern Utah University) where, among his abundant activities, he played college football and acted in Cedar City's world renowned Shakespeare Festival. His theater work continued with acting and stand-in roles in numerous Hollywood movies. The father of six, he was a building contractor, rancher, inventor, postal employee, and president of the Farm Bureau in Kanab, Utah. Ironically, as president of Kanab's Irrigation Commission, he was instrumental in bringing piped irrigation water to Kanab.

Wendel Heaton in the early 1970s. Photo courtesy of Kimber Heaton.

44

In 1984, Wendel and his wife Patsy died in a helicopter crash, leaving their children to grow up in the loving care of relatives. His youngest daughter, Cindy, was 6 years old when she lost her parents, so she was not aware of all the stories her father might have told her siblings. Perhaps he never told this one. She admits, however, that his role in this story "sounds just like something my dad would do."

Though the North Kaibab, River, and Bright Angel are the trails that Wendel and the merry three trudged along together in song and triumph, Muriel, Pat, and Penny will always refer to the entire pathway from rim to rim as Wendel's Trail. They say he's sprinting along down there somewhere, spurring all the errant and foolish hikers onward toward the rim, goading them on with promises of nice ice-cold root beers if they just make it to the next switchback.

The Redwall Bridge at mile-point 3.0

Afterword

The Hikers – Dan, Penny, Monica, Don

On October 10, 2010, also referred to as 10/10/10, four people again headed down the North Kaibab Trail to hike the Grand Canyon. This time however, with one exception, the group differed from the carefree teens that plodded through the adventure you have just read. Penny (70) and her brother Dan (66) left the rim to fulfill Penny's promise to show him the places their father had worked so many years before—the Pump House at Roaring Springs and the nearby Power House. They were accompanied by Penny's husband Don (72) and their daughter Monica (46). In addition, this trip was to be a somewhat-out-of-the-ordinary celebration of two milestone birthdays—Penny's 70th on that very day and her father's 100th exactly 3 months earlier.

Leaving the cool (30°F) canyon rim at 8:00 a.m., their 3,021-foot descent began under a clear blue sky; their destination awaited more than 5 miles away. This hike was much different than the 1958 adventure. Wearing sturdy hiking boots with thick socks, they carried small packs filled with food, first aid, and abundant water.

The trail was significantly steeper than the last time Penny had hiked it. Decades of heavy storms had washed it out in numerous places, and the route had been changed by the addition of several new switchbacks. In addition, budget cuts had resulted in minimal trail maintenance over the years. What had once been a steep yet relatively easy trail had now become a pathway of deeply eroded dirt and rock interrupted by crossbars of large logs bolted into the underlying rock and soil. The crossbars created widely spaced steps that continued for a distance of more than two grueling miles. The deep furrows had been further enlarged by dozens of mules that descend the trail daily during the spring and summer months, and often contain the "droppings" that mules, by their very nature, tend to leave behind.

Webster clan at Kaibab Lodge - Don, Penny, Monica, Dan, Jill

The presence of dozens of hikers along the trail was a big surprise to Penny. In years past, hikers had been sparse except for the brave few who ventured into the depths, and never more than two or three were ever passed on the trail in the same day. Now, it seems hundreds of hikers had discovered the spirit of the canyon and were willing to undertake the arduous trek, making the traverse seem more like a busy freeway than a wilderness trail.

The four descended, each traveling at their own rate of speed, with Penny following by a few dozen yards or even a switchback or two as she favored a newly repaired knee. She hated to think that her age had anything to do with her slower progress. At mile-point 1.7 (Supai Tunnel) she met the rest of her group along with a dozen or so other hikers in varying physical conditions. Many were lying on the rocks to rest before venturing farther up or down. Others were applying dressings to their assorted blisters, and one young hiker with extremely sore leg muscles was being assisted by Penny's brother, who showed her companions how to ease her discomfort as she ascended the remainder of the trail to the North Rim. Two men soon appeared showing signs of extreme fatigue and weakness after hiking across the canyon from the South Rim, and as they described their lack of adequate food, Don gave them a large sack of trail mix that they eagerly accepted. They munched the sugar and other carbohydrates and then lay back on the rocks to gain strength for the final leg of their journey up to the North Rim.

Rounding a bend near Supai Tunnel (see similar photo on page 14)

An even bigger surprise at this point in the trail was the presence of a water fountain, restrooms, shade, and a hitching rail to tether the mules when they arrived. When Penny had last visited this place, the tunnel was the only feature that provided any shade at all to canyon hikers, and water was only a fleeting dream in the minds of weary and thirsty hikers.

They had been resting quite a while when they realized that Penny had disappeared. Upon investigating, they learned that the lock on the restroom door had stuck and she had been unable to open it. Pounding on the door, she was eventually rescued by another hiker who heard the noise and her plea for help. It seems that hiking the canyon still brings out a bit of comedy now and then to balance the adventurous spirit.

Sampling their food and various snacks, the four headed farther down the trail, which by now had become even steeper with still no relief from the sun that blazed high in the sky. The temperature had risen to the high 80s or low 90s, and they longed for any bit of shade they might find.

At about mile-point 2.5, realizing she had traveled slightly less than half way down, Penny reluctantly called it quits and turned around. Time was passing more rapidly than she had expected, and she knew that darkness would be racing her to the rim. Disappointed, she waited until the others were out of sight, and then found an out-of-the-way spot at the corner of a dusty red switchback where she removed her waist pack and found her canteen. Having planned a more formal ceremony with all four of them at Roaring Springs, she alone raised the canteen to the sky as she smiled and then slowly made a series of toasts:

- To her father, who had inadvertently led them all to this place;
- To Wendel, who had triumphantly led a small and daring troop out of it;
- To Muriel, who had enchantingly filled the canyon with songs of youth;
- To Pat, who had comically suffered through potential disaster.

With each sip she paused in silent salute to a long-ago time as she recalled the laughter, the songs, the innocence, the adventure, the rescue, and most of all the friendships that were forever secured. Then she capped her canteen, gathered her gear, and headed back up the trail toward the rim.

At about mile-point 1.5, she heard the familiar sounds of hooves on rock as a long mule train came into view down the trail toward her. Waiting on the inside of the trail she watched each mule pass in front of her and then heard a familiar voice. It was her other daughter, Jill (48), sitting atop a mule as it strode along the trail. Unable to hike the canyon because of impending hip surgery, Jill had decided to commemorate the day in the canyon anyway by riding a mule, hoping to meet up with her family somewhere en route. When Jill spied her mother, she yelled out to the other riders, "Hey everyone, here comes a Webster. It's my mom and she's 70 years old today!" They all whooped and hollered, congratulating Penny on her spirited adventure, and then disappeared around the next switchback heading toward their destination at Supai Tunnel.

In the meantime, Monica and her dad had hiked as far as mile-point 3.0, the new Redwall Bridge across the ravine, and they too decided to turn back. The time was well past noon and they still had over 2 miles to reach their destination before turning around and heading upward the full distance. It was clear that they would not reach Roaring Springs or the Power House and make it out of the canyon before dark. In addition, they had to admit that they were just too tired of the dust, the steepness, and the overall discomfort they were feeling.

The Rider – Jill

51

Dan, however, decided to venture a little farther along the trail, so he waved goodbye and continued on his way. In pursuit of some photos, he followed the trail that leveled out somewhat for about a half mile along the edge of a cliff (see page 14), and then he too made the same decision. He turned around just as the trail again became another series of steep switchbacks in full sun. It was now clear to each of them that attempting a hike of nearly 11 arduous miles in one day had probably not been a great idea, especially on a trail in such condition. Other hikers did it every day but, undoubtedly, most of them were stronger and much younger.

As they ascended at their own pace, they each met up with the mule train to discover that Jill was having a wonderful adventure of her own. Seeing each of them as they awaited trailside for the train to pass, she would holler out, "Here comes another Webster!" As this routine played out over and over again, someone on the train finally asked her, "Just how many of the Webster clan are on the trail today, anyway?" "Oh there are five of us altogether," she replied. Apparently, it was not a routine occurrence to have so many family members in the canyon all at the same time.

The ascent continued as Dan passed Monica and Don, and then passed Penny farther on up the trail. His second wind had kicked in and he was making tracks in good spirits. Monica, however, ran into an unexpected snag. At about one mile from the rim, she became faint and nauseous, and her condition continued intermittently the rest of the way. Catching up with Penny just as she was ending one of her many rest breaks, Monica grew cold and began to shake. She lay back against the limestone at the side of the trail while Penny wrapped her in a down vest to warm her up. Though quite weak, she slowly moved upward, resting every few yards as the symptoms recurred. Then, about a half mile from the top, Don removed Monica's pack from her shoulders and carried it the rest of the way along with his own.

They finally reached the rim of the canyon at about 4:00 p.m. and, coincidentally, Jill's mule team had also just reached the top. They all hugged one another, congratulating themselves on at least attempting to reach their goals in this most unusual celebration. They now understood why this particular section of the trail is considered the most difficult of the three maintained trails in the Grand Canyon. Amidst their jubilation, however, Monica's condition persisted and a park ranger stopped to provide assistance. After medical tests taken later at the ambulance garage, he declared that her physical condition was excellent, but she was "just plain pooped!" A large dose of electrolytic beverage brought relief from the problem, and everyone finally proclaimed the day to have been another grand adventure accented with unexpected events.

Luckily, they had encountered no snakes, no frogs, no skunks, and no bats. Nevertheless, the trek created new family memories to be told and retold in the coming years, and it brought back memories of long ago. In the midst of it all were the inevitable aches, pains, and dramatic episodes associated with a round-trip hike on one of Grand Canyon's many spectacular trails.

Monica on the rim (above) and
Jill at Supai Tunnel (right)

Dan, Monica and Don on the rim

Next time... we'll all cross the bridge and keep on going.

The following day, standing on the edge of the canyon, Penny sighed deeply as she gazed back into the depths one more time. She stared quietly for a few moments and then looked down at her dusty shoes. "Hmmm," she thought to herself as a smile formed on her lips and a new thought entered her mind, "I wonder how far I can go on my 80th?"

Penny at Point Imperial

Printed in the United States
By Bookmasters